Unlocking the Power of Cursor AI

Code Smarter, Not Harder—The Ultimate Tool for Next-Gen Developers

TABLE OF CONTENTS

- The Future of Development is Now: Take Control with Cursor AI

- Embrace AI and Transform Your Coding Career

INTRODUCTION

In the fast-evolving world of software development, one thing is certain: the tools developers use shape not just the products they create but the very nature of the work itself. It's no longer just about writing code; it's about optimizing the process, refining the workflow, and leveraging every advantage available. Enter Cursor AI, a revolutionary tool poised to redefine the way developers interact with their code. This book aims to guide you through this transformative tool and help you understand why Cursor AI is not just another trend, but a game-changer in the software development landscape.

The digital age has brought with it an unparalleled speed of innovation, and as the complexity of the systems developers work on increases, so too must their methods and tools. In the past, software development was marked by trial and error, long debugging sessions, and manual coding. It was, to some extent, a solitary effort — a one-man or one-woman job. Yet, as technology progressed, so did the expectations placed on developers. Today, they are not only expected to write flawless code but to do so with an efficiency and speed that wasn't possible before. In a world where software is expected to be built faster, with fewer bugs, and with greater scalability, developers are left to wonder: How do we keep up?

The answer, in large part, lies in AI. With the advent of artificial intelligence, developers now have access to powerful tools that streamline their work, identify potential issues before they arise, and even assist in writing code faster. But not all AI tools are created equal. Some are designed as basic assistants, offering minor conveniences.

Others, like Cursor AI, stand apart as powerful enablers that redefine what's possible in modern software development.

> Why Cursor AI is a Game-Changer for Developers

What sets Cursor AI apart from other tools is its unique ability to seamlessly integrate into the development process, offering assistance not as an external, separate tool but as an integral part of the coding experience. It doesn't just automate basic tasks — it elevates the entire process. It's not about replacing developers, but about augmenting their abilities to create faster, more accurate, and more efficient code.

Consider this: many developers have spent countless hours debugging, refactoring, and testing their code to meet the standards of their projects. While these tasks are essential, they are often time-consuming and repetitive. This is where Cursor AI comes in. Instead of developers being bogged down by the minutiae, Cursor AI helps identify errors before they even occur, suggesting corrections as the code is being written. It automates tedious tasks, allowing developers to focus on what truly matters: solving complex problems, creating innovative features, and enhancing the user experience.

Furthermore, Cursor AI is not limited to just individual code corrections. It's an intelligent system that understands the broader context of the code, offering suggestions for entire blocks of code, refactoring suggestions, and even creating code snippets that fit seamlessly into the developer's project. This proactive approach is a significant step forward in the way developers interact with their code. Instead of waiting for errors to appear and then fixing them, developers can now be guided in real-time, with Cursor AI offering helpful suggestions every step of the way.

Cursor AI is also a powerful tool for collaboration. In today's software development environment, developers are often working on large teams, spread across various time zones, with complex codebases to manage. Cursor AI's ability to provide consistent, AI-driven suggestions for everyone in the team helps ensure that the code remains clean, efficient, and consistent across the board. For team leads and managers, this can make a world of difference, as it helps maintain coding standards and facilitates a more streamlined development process.

The impact of Cursor AI extends beyond just the efficiency of coding. As developers work to keep up with the rapid advancements in technology, there's an increasing need to future-proof their careers. By incorporating

AI-powered tools like Cursor AI into their daily workflows, developers can stay ahead of the curve. They become part of the new wave of professionals who not only know how to write code but also understand how to harness the power of AI to improve their coding practices. In this sense, Cursor AI is not just a tool for the present, but an investment in the future of development.

> How This Book Will Help You Code Smarter, Not Harder

This book is designed to help you harness the full potential of Cursor AI in your coding journey. It is a practical guide, aimed at developers of all levels, from beginners to seasoned professionals, who want to streamline their development process and enhance their productivity. With a step-by-step approach, this book will show you how to integrate Cursor AI into your daily workflow, allowing you to work smarter, not harder.

If you're new to the world of development or have never used AI-powered tools before, don't worry. This book will introduce you to Cursor AI in an accessible, straightforward way. We'll walk you through the basics — from installing the software to understanding the core features — and provide easy-to-follow instructions that will help you get up and running in no time. By the end of this book, you'll not only be able to use Cursor AI with confidence but also fully appreciate how it can make a tangible difference in your coding efficiency. For more experienced developers, this book will delve deeper into the advanced capabilities of Cursor AI. You'll learn how to use the tool to unlock complex features like automated debugging, smart code suggestions, and enhanced refactoring tools. This book will guide you through real-world examples and case studies, demonstrating how leading companies use Cursor AI to build better, faster, and more efficient software. By integrating these techniques into your own workflow, you can elevate your coding game to new heights.

At the heart of this book is the belief that you should never settle for just good enough. Cursor AI is not a tool for simply automating mundane tasks; it's a tool for supercharging your development process. The goal is to empower you with the knowledge and skills to write better code, more efficiently, while maintaining the control and precision that you need as a developer. This book will help you unlock the full potential of Cursor AI, transforming the way you approach coding.

In a world that demands faster delivery times, more complex features, and higher standards, Cursor AI provides the edge developers need to keep up. It doesn't just make coding easier; it makes it smarter. And in the end, that's what separates the best developers from the rest. By mastering Cursor AI, you'll not only be able to meet the demands of today's fast-paced software development world but also ensure that you're well-equipped to tackle the challenges of tomorrow.

This is your opportunity to not just learn a new tool, but to transform the way you work. With the guidance provided in this book, you'll soon realize that the future of development is not about working harder — it's about working smarter. And with Cursor AI, the future is now.

CHAPTER ONE

Getting Started with Cursor AI

In the ever-evolving world of software development, new tools and innovations emerge almost daily. Yet, few advancements hold the transformative potential that artificial intelligence (AI) brings to the coding world. Among the most groundbreaking of these tools is Cursor AI, a platform designed to significantly enhance the coding experience for developers. Whether you're a seasoned coder or just beginning, Cursor AI offers something for everyone. But as with any tool, knowing how to set it up and navigate its features is crucial to unlocking its true power.

> Introduction to Cursor AI

Cursor AI is not simply another code editor or IDE (integrated development environment). It is, in essence, a productivity enhancer, designed to assist developers by automating mundane tasks and providing intelligent insights into their work. The AI capabilities embedded within Cursor AI allow it to make code suggestions, automatically detect errors, and optimize repetitive processes. It acts not as a replacement for developers but as a companion, enhancing their efficiency while maintaining the human touch that remains essential in coding.

Unlike traditional coding tools that focus only on providing a platform to write code, Cursor AI takes it a step further by integrating powerful AI to predict, suggest, and even generate parts of the code based on patterns. It aims to reduce time spent on routine tasks like debugging, error-checking, and even documentation, allowing developers to focus more on creative and complex problem-solving.

For a developer, the value lies in its ability to learn and adapt to your style over time, making it feel like a personalized assistant. It's a tool that gets smarter the more you use it, learning from the structure of your code and improving its suggestions. Whether you're working on a small project or managing a complex, multi-layered application, Cursor AI promises to streamline the process and make development smoother.

> Setting Up and Installing Cursor AI

The first step in harnessing the power of Cursor AI is setting it up. The installation process is straightforward, ensuring even novice users won't feel overwhelmed. Unlike some software that requires intricate knowledge of system configurations, Cursor AI's setup is user-friendly, designed to cater to those with varying levels of technical expertise.

1. Download and Installation

To begin, download the Cursor AI installer from the official website or repository. The installer is available for various platforms—Windows, macOS, and Linux—ensuring that developers across different ecosystems can access the tool. Upon downloading, you'll be prompted to run the installation wizard. This step is simple: you'll choose your installation directory, confirm the necessary permissions, and proceed with the installation process.

2. Dependencies and Environment Setup

Before jumping into coding, it's essential to ensure that all necessary dependencies are correctly set up. Cursor AI integrates seamlessly with popular code editors and IDEs such as Visual Studio Code, JetBrains, and Sublime Text. During installation, the tool will check for any missing dependencies and offer suggestions for what needs to be installed. In most cases, this process is automated, but in rare instances, the user may be prompted to manually install certain plugins or extensions.

3. Account Setup and Configuration

Once installed, users are encouraged to create an account or sign in to an existing one. While using Cursor AI does not mandate an account, creating one enables synchronization of settings across multiple devices. This is particularly useful for developers who switch between machines or work on collaborative projects. Cursor AI allows users to configure their environment settings, such as preferred coding languages, theme (light or dark), and keyboard shortcuts. By customizing these settings, the platform becomes more aligned with your working preferences, increasing overall productivity.

4. Connecting with Version Control

One of the key benefits of Cursor AI is its seamless integration with version control systems, such as Git. Upon setup, the tool will prompt users to link their repositories, ensuring that changes are tracked and can be easily committed. This integration enhances the development process by ensuring that AI-generated code remains consistent with the rest of the project's development history.

5. Initial Test Run

After the setup is complete, it's always a good idea to run a quick test. Open your code editor, activate Cursor AI, and start typing. The tool should immediately begin suggesting code completions, identifying syntax errors, or offering refactor recommendations. This initial interaction provides a sense of how the tool works and what improvements can be expected from its use.

> Navigating the Interface: What You Need to Know

While the installation process is fairly simple, understanding how to navigate Cursor AI's interface is essential for making the most of its features. The interface is designed with the user in mind, offering intuitive access to the most important features while keeping the workspace uncluttered. Below are the key elements to familiarize yourself with as you begin using Cursor AI.

1. Code Suggestions and Autocompletion

The primary feature of Cursor AI is its intelligent code suggestions. As you type, the tool offers autocompletions based on its understanding of the project and the code patterns you've used before. These suggestions aren't just limited to syntax—Cursor AI can suggest entire functions or classes based on the context. The more you use it, the better it gets at predicting your needs. The suggestions appear in a dropdown, making them easy to select, but also allowing you to continue typing if you prefer to write the code yourself.

2. Error Detection and Debugging

Another standout feature is the real-time error detection. Unlike traditional code editors that only highlight syntax issues, Cursor AI takes this a step further by recognizing potential logical or runtime errors. When an issue is detected, the tool flags it and offers suggestions for how to resolve it. The errors are color-coded, and a quick click on the error will open a helpful explanation or troubleshooting guide. This feature is invaluable for both beginners and experienced developers, ensuring that issues are caught early in the development process.

3. Refactoring and Code Cleanup

As you work through your code, Cursor AI will often suggest refactorings to improve code readability and efficiency. These suggestions range from simple changes, such as renaming variables for clarity, to more complex adjustments like breaking large functions into smaller, reusable components. While the tool does not impose these changes on the developer, it provides easy-to-accept suggestions, allowing you to clean up your code quickly without interrupting your workflow.

4. Project Navigation

Cursor AI includes a feature to navigate large codebases with ease. In traditional environments, searching for a function or class within a massive project can be time-consuming. With Cursor AI, you can instantly jump to any function, class, or variable simply by typing its name or using keyboard shortcuts. This feature streamlines navigation, saving you time and frustration when working on complex applications with multiple files.

5. Integration with Documentation and Tutorials

Finally, Cursor AI offers helpful built-in documentation and tutorials. When you're unfamiliar with a function or library, the tool can link directly to its documentation, ensuring that you have all the information you need to use it correctly. For beginners, this feature is an excellent way to learn as you go, making the learning curve much less steep.

> A Deeper Dive into the Features

While the installation and initial setup are the first steps toward mastering Cursor AI, the true power of this tool lies in its nuanced features that can take your development workflow to the next level. For developers, whether beginners or experienced, understanding how to leverage Cursor AI's unique functionalities is key to enhancing productivity, improving code quality, and ultimately speeding up development.

Enhanced Code Suggestions

One of the most compelling aspects of Cursor AI is its smart code suggestion system. As you begin typing, Cursor AI does more than just offer autocompletions based on simple keyword matching. The AI analyzes your existing codebase, considers the context of your current function, and suggests relevant code snippets or entire functions based on these factors.

For example, if you're working in Python and are typing a function that requires a list operation, Cursor AI will suggest methods that are commonly used with lists, such as `append()` or `extend()`. As your project progresses, the AI will adapt to your coding patterns and make increasingly accurate suggestions, making it feel like a custom-built assistant. What sets this feature apart from basic autocompletion is its ability to suggest code based on your coding style. If you're more inclined to use concise one-liners, the AI will recognize that and provide suggestions that fit your preference.

Conversely, if you prefer a more verbose or structured approach, it will align with that style too. This dynamic suggestion system allows Cursor AI to blend seamlessly with your workflow, minimizing friction while maximizing efficiency.

> Smart Error Detection and Troubleshooting

A critical part of development is the process of debugging and troubleshooting. One of the most frustrating experiences for developers is the realization that a bug has remained undetected for too long, only to disrupt production at the worst possible time. Cursor AI's error detection system addresses this issue head-on by actively scanning your code as you write, flagging any errors or issues that could potentially break your application.

Unlike traditional error detection, which focuses primarily on syntax errors, Cursor AI goes a step further by analyzing the logic of your code. If there's an inconsistency in how you've structured a loop or a function, Cursor AI will flag it and offer suggestions for correcting it. For instance, if you have a function with an unhandled edge case, the tool will point this out and provide recommendations for improving your logic. Moreover, Cursor AI also comes equipped with real-time fix suggestions that developers can implement with a single click. These fixes are generated by the AI and are based on a comprehensive understanding of best practices for various programming languages. This proactive approach to error management helps prevent bugs from reaching the later stages of development or, worse, production.

> Refactoring Your Code for Greater Efficiency

Code refactoring is an integral part of development that ensures your application remains scalable, maintainable, and efficient. While developers may understand the importance of refactoring, it can often be a time-consuming and tedious process. With Cursor AI, this task becomes automated and much less overwhelming.

As you work through your code, Cursor AI continuously analyzes the structure of your functions, methods, and classes. If it detects an opportunity for improvement—whether it's renaming variables for clarity, breaking large functions into smaller, more manageable ones, or optimizing performance—it will suggest these changes. These suggestions are not imposed but are presented in an easily digestible format, allowing you to decide whether or not to implement them. For example, if a function becomes too lengthy or convoluted, Cursor AI might suggest breaking it up into smaller, more focused functions. Similarly, if you have redundant code blocks, the AI will recommend consolidating them into a single function or method. These kinds of refactorings often lead to more efficient code that is easier to maintain and scale, especially when working in larger teams or on complex projects.

> Seamless Project Navigation

As any developer knows, navigating large codebases can be a nightmare. Searching through hundreds, if not thousands, of lines of code can be an exhausting and time-consuming process, especially when trying to find a specific function or class. Cursor AI alleviates this problem by offering instant search and navigation capabilities.

By typing the name of a function, class, or variable into the search bar, you can instantly jump to the part of the code that you need, without having to sift through the entire project. This feature allows you to keep your focus where it matters most—on the actual coding and problem-solving—without getting bogged down in the logistics of finding the correct lines of code.

In addition, Cursor AI also offers a contextual navigation feature, meaning that as you move through your project, it will suggest relevant sections of code to check based on what you're currently working on. For example, if you're editing a function that interacts with a database, Cursor AI might suggest navigating to the section where database connections are initialized, allowing you to easily see the broader context in which your code operates.

> Leveraging AI for Documentation and Learning

Writing documentation is often an afterthought for many developers, and yet it is one of the most critical aspects of long-term software maintenance. Cursor AI helps bridge this gap by automatically generating documentation as you code. This documentation is based on the function and variable names you use, as well as the comments you add to your code. By intelligently analyzing the code, Cursor AI can suggest or even generate detailed descriptions of what each part of your code is doing, saving you from the time-consuming task of writing everything manually.

Additionally, Cursor AI's integration with online documentation resources means that you can easily reference and learn from the best coding practices without leaving your IDE. Whether you're working with a new library or API, the tool can link you directly to the official documentation for quick reference, ensuring that you're always coding in line with best practices.

> Customizing Cursor AI to Fit Your Workflow

As powerful as Cursor AI is out of the box, its true potential shines when you personalize it to fit your specific development needs. The platform allows you to adjust a wide range of settings, from the types of code suggestions you receive to the look and feel of the interface. You can tailor the AI's behavior to be more or less aggressive in suggesting fixes, allowing you to strike a balance between guidance and freedom. You can also integrate third-party tools, plugins, and extensions to further enhance your workflow, depending on the languages and frameworks you use. This level of customization ensures that Cursor AI adapts to your coding style, rather than forcing you to adapt to the tool.

The first chapter of mastering Cursor AI is just the beginning. With its powerful code suggestions, real-time error detection, refactoring tools, and seamless navigation, it has the potential to completely transform how you approach software development. By integrating this AI tool into your workflow, you can reduce the time spent on repetitive tasks, minimize human error, and ultimately write cleaner, more efficient code.

As you continue exploring its capabilities, you'll find that Cursor AI is more than just a tool; it's a powerful assistant that can grow with you and your projects. With time and experience, you'll learn to rely on it to handle the mundane aspects of development, freeing you to focus on the creative, problem-solving parts of coding that truly define your work. And with every passing project, your productivity, efficiency, and coding quality will continue to improve.

CHAPTER TWO

AI for Beginners: Mastering the Basics

In the landscape of modern software development, one of the most compelling advancements in recent years has been the integration of artificial intelligence (AI) into coding processes. AI-powered coding represents a major leap forward, streamlining how developers create, debug, and optimize their code. This chapter serves as an introduction to the world of AI-assisted development, with a particular focus on Cursor AI. For beginners, understanding the fundamentals of AI-driven development tools is essential, as these technologies promise not only to enhance productivity but also to improve the quality of the code itself.

> Understanding AI-Powered Coding

At its core, AI-powered coding tools like Cursor AI aim to assist developers by making intelligent suggestions, automating repetitive tasks, and detecting errors in real-time. But before diving into the specific features of Cursor AI, it's important to understand how AI, in general, plays a role in the world of software development.

AI has been designed to mimic the decision-making abilities of humans. In software development, this means that AI can analyze patterns in code and suggest or generate code that fits with those patterns. This is in stark contrast to traditional coding tools, which typically only help with syntax, error highlighting, and basic autocomplete features. AI, on the other hand, uses advanced machine learning algorithms to predict what the developer might need next, based on an understanding of the context, structure, and flow of the project.

While traditional tools focus mainly on offering autocompletions for individual lines of code, AI tools like Cursor AI go a step further. These tools can analyze entire codebases, identify potential issues, and provide smart, context-sensitive suggestions that help the developer write better code more quickly. This is especially valuable for beginners, who might struggle with writing optimized or error-free code on their own. By offering instant feedback and guidance, Cursor AI helps developers learn best practices as they go. For example, if you were writing a Python function to fetch data from an API, Cursor AI might suggest the most efficient way to handle HTTP requests based on the specific context of the function. It could even help format the function according to best practices, or suggest error handling mechanisms that you may not have thought of.

AI's role in coding is ultimately about augmentation, not replacement. It doesn't replace the need for human creativity and decision-making but rather enhances the developer's capabilities, allowing them to focus on the bigger picture while the tool handles the repetitive and mundane tasks. Understanding how AI can complement your work is the first step in embracing this transformative technology.

> How to Use Cursor AI for Your First Project

Now that we've established what AI-powered coding can do, let's turn our attention to how to use Cursor AI effectively for your first project. While some tools may require a steep learning curve, Cursor AI is designed with simplicity in mind, especially for beginners.

● Setting Up for Success

Before you begin, the first thing you need to do is ensure that Cursor AI is installed and properly set up. As we covered in the previous chapter, installation is a straightforward process, so let's focus on what you'll do once it's up and running.

When you first launch Cursor AI, you'll notice a familiar environment—whether you're using Visual Studio Code, JetBrains, or another editor, Cursor AI integrates seamlessly into these platforms. You won't have to learn an entirely new interface. Once installed, the tool will begin analyzing your current project and the code you've written so far, providing smart code suggestions right from the start.

Starting Your First Project with Cursor AI

For a beginner, it's helpful to start with a small, manageable project that will give you a hands-on understanding of how Cursor AI works. A simple task could be building a basic calculator app in Python, JavaScript, or another language you are comfortable with.

1. Create a New Project

Open your chosen code editor and create a new project. For example, if you're building a calculator, create a new Python file (e.g., `calculator.py`).

2. Activate Cursor AI

Once your project is open, ensure that Cursor AI is activated in your editor. It may appear as a sidebar or an integrated feature in the editor itself. From here, you'll have access to its full suite of features, from code suggestions to error detection.

3. Write Your First Function

Begin by writing your first function. In the case of the calculator, you might start with a simple addition function like this:

```python
def add(x, y):

    return x + y
```

As soon as you begin typing, Cursor AI will likely offer suggestions, such as formatting, variable naming improvements, or additional optimizations. For example, it might suggest using type hints in Python for better readability:

```python
def add(x: int, y: int) -> int:
```

```
    return x + y

```

As a beginner, these subtle improvements might not always be intuitive, but Cursor AI will guide you towards writing more efficient and readable code.

4. Use Cursor AI's Autocomplete and Suggestions

As you continue to add more functions (e.g., subtract, multiply, divide), Cursor AI will continuously offer context-aware suggestions. For instance, if you start typing a function like `subtract`, Cursor AI will suggest the full function signature, and may even offer improvements based on similar code patterns it has learned from other developers.

5. Refactor Code with Cursor AI's Help

As your project grows, you'll find that your initial code might become less organized. Refactoring code is an essential part of software development, and Cursor AI makes this process painless. For example, it might suggest breaking your calculator functions into separate classes or organizing related functionality into modules. These recommendations will help you improve the scalability of your code.

6. Testing Your Code

After you've written a few functions, testing becomes important. For beginners, writing test cases may feel like an extra chore, but Cursor AI can simplify this by automatically generating tests for you based on your functions. If you've written a function like `add(x, y)`, Cursor AI could suggest a corresponding test case, such as:

```python
def test_add():

    assert add(2, 3) == 5
```

This process ensures that the basic functionality of your code is working correctly and will alert you to any problems as your project grows.

> Real-Time Debugging

Debugging is an inevitable part of the coding process, but Cursor AI makes it easier. As you work, Cursor AI will detect logical errors, bugs, or even inefficient patterns in real time. For example, if you forget to handle edge cases (e.g., division by zero in a division function), Cursor AI will flag this issue and recommend an appropriate solution.

What makes Cursor AI even more powerful is its ability to understand the logic behind your code. So, if you're trying to implement a feature like user input validation, Cursor AI can suggest methods that prevent potential bugs before they happen, saving you time and effort in the debugging phase.

> Simple Code Enhancements with Cursor AI

Now that you understand how to start a project, let's take a look at how Cursor AI can help improve your code with simple enhancements. As you progress through your coding journey, these enhancements will become increasingly valuable.

Auto-Refactoring for Clean Code

Cursor AI helps you maintain clean and maintainable code. It can detect redundancies and suggest how to streamline your codebase. For example, if you have multiple functions performing similar tasks, Cursor AI might suggest combining them into a more efficient structure.

For instance, let's say you have two functions like this:

```python
def multiply(x, y):
    return x * y


def divide(x, y):
    return x / y
```

Both functions contain repeated code. Cursor AI might suggest combining them into a single, more efficient function. This process improves readability and minimizes code duplication, which is essential for scalability.

> Improving Code Readability

Beginners often write functional code that works but lacks clarity or proper structure. Cursor AI can suggest improvements to your code that will make it easier for others (or yourself in the future) to understand. It could recommend adding comments, adjusting variable names, or restructuring code for better flow.

For example, if your function names are too vague or general, Cursor AI might suggest more descriptive alternatives:

```python
def calc(x, y):
```

```
    return x + y
```

Cursor AI might suggest:

```python
def add_numbers(x: int, y: int) -> int:
    return x + y
```

This change improves the function's clarity, making it more understandable to other developers or even your future self.

Mastering AI-powered coding tools like Cursor AI can be a game-changer for any developer, but particularly for beginners. By using AI to assist in coding, error detection, and refactoring, you can drastically reduce the time spent on debugging and focus more on creating innovative solutions. As you continue to use Cursor AI in your development work, you'll find that it not only saves you time but also helps you become a better developer.

The key to successfully integrating Cursor AI into your development process is starting small, learning how to use the tool effectively, and gradually exploring its more advanced features as you grow more comfortable. With practice, Cursor AI will become a seamless part of your workflow, guiding you to write clean, efficient, and error-free code, every time.

CHAPTER THREE

Streamlining Your Development Workflow

For decades, developers have been on a relentless pursuit to make their work more efficient, more precise, and ultimately faster. With every technological leap, new tools and frameworks have emerged, each promising to ease the burdens of coding, debugging, and testing. Yet, even with all the advancements, a central challenge remains: how can a developer manage the relentless tide of repetitive tasks and intricate details that bog down the creative process?

The answer to that question, for many, has arrived in the form of Cursor AI, an intelligent tool designed not just to assist, but to accelerate the development process by automating mundane tasks, enhancing decision-making, and offering intelligent insights that smoothen the coding journey. This chapter explores how Cursor AI helps developers streamline their workflow by automating repetitive coding tasks, speeding up code writing through smart suggestions, and offering time-saving tips that ultimately empower developers to do more with less effort.

> Automating Repetitive Coding Tasks

One of the primary obstacles developers face is the sheer volume of repetitive tasks required to get a program from an idea to a finished product. Coding, by its very nature, can be a meticulous process—one that often requires the developer to write similar code blocks over and over again, whether it's for handling user input, creating new classes, or building the logic of basic functions. These tasks are necessary but time-consuming, and the act of repeating them can be a drain on both productivity and creativity.

Enter Cursor AI.

Cursor AI's automation capabilities focus on reducing the time spent on these repetitive coding tasks. For example, imagine you are building an application that requires multiple forms for user input. Without Cursor AI, you would likely write similar validation code for each input field, perhaps needing to define functions for validating email addresses, passwords, phone numbers, and so on. The effort required to write, check, and refactor this code can add up quickly, consuming precious time that could be better spent elsewhere.

With Cursor AI, this process becomes vastly more efficient. The tool recognizes these repetitive patterns and offers suggestions for automated code generation, which reduces the need to write redundant functions manually. Instead of reinventing the wheel each time, Cursor AI generates the required code for validation and similar tasks, streamlining the entire process and saving you hours of manual labor. This automation is one of the key features that make Cursor AI so appealing to developers at all levels.

Furthermore, Cursor AI doesn't just automate code generation; it improves consistency across the application. When you let the AI handle these repetitive tasks, you ensure that the same principles and best practices are applied uniformly, reducing human error and maintaining a high standard of quality throughout the project.

> **Speeding Up Code Writing with Cursor AI's Smart Suggestions**

For all its strengths, writing code manually is inherently a slow and iterative process. The challenge is not necessarily in understanding the logic or structure of a program, but in the act of typing the code, reviewing it, and correcting errors.

Cursor AI tackles this challenge head-on with its smart suggestions—an intelligent system designed to predict and offer code completions that match the developer's intent. As you start typing, Cursor AI quickly analyzes the surrounding context and suggests the next logical steps. This feature is far more than a mere autocomplete function; it understands the syntax, the libraries you're working with, and the project structure.

For example, imagine you are working on a Python project and need to write a function that parses data from an external JSON file. With traditional tools, you would have to look up how to parse the data, figure out the correct syntax, and manually write out each line. Cursor AI, however, will suggest the most efficient way to handle the operation, offering you code snippets such as:

```python
import json

def parse_json(file_path):
    with open(file_path, 'r') as f:
        data = json.load(f)
    return data
```

These suggestions come with an understanding of your coding habits—if you consistently use certain libraries or patterns, Cursor AI adapts to your preferences and suggests solutions that are increasingly aligned with your approach. This saves the developer considerable time by reducing the cognitive load required to recall syntax or figure out the optimal approach to solving a problem.

Moreover, as your project progresses, Cursor AI's suggestions become even more precise. If you're working on a complex function and your code reaches a certain level of complexity, Cursor AI can suggest refactors, break down functions into smaller components, or propose alternate methods that would improve both performance and clarity. The faster you write code, the more quickly you move from problem to solution, and Cursor AI helps accelerate this transition by suggesting solutions that are contextually relevant.

> **Time-Saving Tips for Everyday Tasks**

A significant portion of a developer's time isn't spent on building new features, but rather on handling the minutiae—the maintenance, debugging, testing, and refactoring that ensure the software remains functional and performant. These tasks, while important, are often time-consuming and tedious. Cursor AI excels in providing tips and shortcuts for handling these everyday tasks, allowing developers to free up valuable time for more creative endeavors.

1. Simplifying Debugging with Real-Time Error Detection

One of the most time-consuming aspects of coding is debugging. As every developer knows, finding and fixing errors can be an arduous process—particularly when the bug isn't obvious, or the codebase is large. With Cursor AI, debugging becomes less of a guessing game. The tool constantly monitors your code for potential errors, flagging issues in real-time. It doesn't just point out syntax problems, either; Cursor AI identifies logical errors or potential bottlenecks that could affect performance.

For instance, if you accidentally forget to check for edge cases in your code, Cursor AI might point it out before the code even reaches the testing phase. Rather than spending hours tracking down subtle bugs, you can fix them in real-time, as they arise. This shift in how developers approach debugging drastically reduces the overall time spent on fixing problems and allows for a more efficient and streamlined development process.

2. Streamlined Testing with Auto-Test Generation

Testing is another area where developers often waste significant time. Manually writing test cases, especially for complex applications, can be tedious and repetitive. Cursor AI speeds up this process by automatically generating unit tests for your functions as you work. If you write a function for a new feature, the AI will suggest the most common test cases for that function based on its structure and expected output.

For example, if you've written a function to calculate the average of a set of numbers, Cursor AI might automatically generate tests like:

```python
def test_average():
    assert average([1, 2, 3]) == 2
```

```
assert average([5, 5, 5, 5]) == 5

assert average([10, 20, 30]) == 20
```
```

By automatically generating tests like this, Cursor AI helps you ensure that your code is functioning as expected without requiring you to manually write each individual test case. This not only saves time but also helps to increase code coverage, reducing the risk of bugs in the final product.

### 3. Optimizing Code for Efficiency

Writing efficient code is a vital skill, and one that can sometimes be overlooked in favor of getting the job done. With Cursor AI, efficiency is built into the development process. As you write code, the tool will suggest optimizations for improving performance, reducing memory usage, or simplifying complex code paths.
```

If, for example, you're writing a loop that performs a simple operation multiple times, Cursor AI might suggest using a more efficient method, like a list comprehension in Python, which is faster and more memory-efficient. These suggestions help ensure that the code you write not only works but does so with optimal performance.

Cursor AI is much more than just a tool—it's an intelligent assistant that transforms the way developers work. By automating repetitive tasks, speeding up the code-writing process with smart suggestions, and offering time-saving tips for everyday tasks, Cursor AI allows developers to focus on what really matters: creating innovative and impactful software.

As developers, we are constantly seeking ways to improve our efficiency without sacrificing quality. With Cursor AI, that goal becomes much more achievable. As you continue to incorporate this tool into your workflow, you'll find that the time saved on mundane tasks can be reinvested into more meaningful and creative aspects of development. The future of software development is not just faster and more efficient; it's smarter, and with Cursor AI, you are at the forefront of this transformation.

CHAPTER FOUR

Advanced AI Features for Experienced Developers

For experienced developers, the tools and technologies that once seemed like novelties evolve into essential elements of their daily workflow. Over time, the intricacies of coding shift from basic syntax mastery to the complexities of creating robust, efficient, and scalable software. In this stage of development, developers begin to appreciate tools that do more than just assist in writing code; they seek tools that help them enhance the architecture of their applications, optimize performance, and ensure quality control at every step of the process.

As software development grows in complexity, Cursor AI becomes not just a tool, but a powerful ally in refining the development process. For those with more experience, the value of Cursor AI is in its ability to unlock advanced features that go beyond simple code suggestions. It allows developers to address deeper problems, such as debugging complex code before it breaks production, refactoring inefficient or messy code, and optimizing for both performance and readability. In this chapter, we will explore how experienced developers can leverage these sophisticated features of Cursor AI to streamline their workflow and elevate the quality of their software.

> Unlocking Complex AI Features

For beginners, Cursor AI offers suggestions and simplifications that help them get started. But for seasoned developers, the true power of the tool lies in its ability to handle complex, multifaceted problems. Cursor AI can understand a project's broader structure, enabling it to make decisions based on the context of an entire codebase. The AI doesn't just look at isolated lines of code but is aware of how functions interact, how data flows through the system, and how external libraries or APIs fit into the overall project. One of the most significant features available to advanced users is Context-Aware Code Suggestions. Instead of just predicting what function comes next based on the last few lines of code, Cursor AI takes a more holistic approach. It understands dependencies between modules, the structure of classes and objects, and even your personal coding style. This means that as an experienced developer, you can write complex applications while still receiving helpful suggestions from Cursor AI that fit perfectly into the overall design of your project.

> Understanding Dependencies and Relationships

When you are dealing with a large codebase, one of the most difficult challenges is managing dependencies between different parts of the code. Whether it's tracking the state of data passed through several functions or keeping track of where a certain variable is modified, experienced developers know that managing this complexity can become a massive headache.

Cursor AI simplifies this problem by providing intelligent dependency management. As you work on large-scale projects, Cursor AI identifies the relationships between various modules, functions, and classes. It helps ensure that the right methods are called in the right order, and it keeps an eye out for potential mistakes—such as calling a function before its required data is available. For instance, if you were writing a complex data pipeline that involves pulling data from multiple sources, Cursor AI might suggest ways to sequence those data retrieval functions, alert you to missing error handling, and optimize your data parsing approach.

> Code Refactoring Suggestions

Refactoring is an essential skill for any developer, but it becomes especially important as the complexity of your projects increases. Writing clean, maintainable code is crucial for long-term success, particularly when collaborating with other developers. As systems scale, codebases inevitably become more cluttered with redundant functions, convoluted logic, and outdated patterns. Cursor AI helps experienced developers identify these problem areas and suggest ways to refactor the code for clarity and efficiency.

For example, let's say you're working on a Python project with dozens of utility functions that perform similar tasks—such as validating user input or formatting data. Rather than manually combing through the code to consolidate these functions, Cursor AI can analyze your code and suggest consolidations, renamings, and refactors. It might point out where redundant code can be replaced with more efficient patterns, or where a function could be broken down into smaller, more modular components. These refactoring suggestions can save a significant amount of time and effort, allowing you to focus on implementing new features rather than cleaning up old code. For an experienced developer, refactoring isn't just about making the code "look better"—it's about ensuring that your code can handle future growth without breaking down. Cursor AI doesn't just focus on style improvements; it helps identify areas where performance could be better optimized, ensuring that your code remains efficient even as the project evolves.

> Debugging Code Before It Breaks Production

As projects grow in complexity, the likelihood of encountering bugs increases exponentially. Debugging is a crucial part of the development process, but it's often a time-consuming and frustrating task. For experienced developers, debugging isn't just about fixing issues—it's about identifying potential problems before they escalate and ensuring that the code is robust enough to handle real-world use cases.

One of the standout features of Cursor AI is its proactive error detection capabilities. Rather than waiting for a bug to surface in production or during testing, Cursor AI continuously scans your code in real-time, identifying potential issues as you write. For instance, if you're writing a function that parses data from a web API, Cursor AI will flag potential errors such as improper data handling, unanticipated edge cases, or poor error reporting. It might suggest validation checks for missing data, recommend better error messages, or even highlight inefficient data processing patterns that could cause performance issues under load.

This proactive debugging capability is especially powerful in high-stakes development environments where bugs can cost time, money, or reputation. Cursor AI helps experienced developers catch issues before they escalate, ensuring that potential problems are identified early in the development process, long before they can break production.

> Real-Time Feedback and Resolution Suggestions

What makes Cursor AI's debugging even more powerful is its ability to provide real-time feedback and resolution suggestions. As you write or modify code, the tool actively monitors for issues and offers targeted recommendations. Instead of requiring you to search through logs, stack traces, or error reports, Cursor AI integrates directly into your development environment and highlights potential errors as you work.

For example, if you introduce a bug related to concurrency in a multithreaded application, Cursor AI will identify potential race conditions, deadlocks, or other threading issues. The AI will then provide suggestions on how to resolve those issues, such as recommending thread synchronization mechanisms or introducing new locking techniques to prevent data corruption.

This real-time, intelligent feedback not only saves time but also increases the quality of your code. By addressing errors early, you can focus on the higher-level logic of your application instead of spending hours troubleshooting issues that could have been caught earlier.

> **Refactoring and Optimizing with Cursor AI**

Refactoring and optimizing code are two of the most critical aspects of maintaining a high-quality software project. As the codebase expands, the chances of inefficient, redundant, or unoptimized code increase. Whether it's through better memory management, more efficient algorithms, or cleaner logic, optimizing code is essential for delivering high-performance applications that scale well.

Cursor AI helps experienced developers identify areas for optimization that they may not have noticed. Through its intelligent analysis of code structure, it suggests improvements based on best practices and the context of the project. This could involve offering alternative implementations for specific algorithms, recommending more efficient data structures, or identifying redundant logic that could be eliminated.

Let's say you're working on an algorithm that processes large datasets. Cursor AI can suggest ways to improve its time complexity or memory consumption. If your code is unnecessarily iterating over large datasets multiple times, Cursor AI might recommend caching intermediate results or refactoring your logic to process the data in a more efficient manner.

> **Advanced Performance Optimization**

Optimizing for performance is a critical concern for experienced developers, especially when working on resource-intensive applications such as large-scale web services, games, or data processing pipelines. Cursor AI supports developers by recommending performance optimizations based on a deep understanding of both the underlying code and the system architecture. For example, if you're working with a database-heavy application, Cursor AI might suggest optimizations like using batch processing for database queries instead of individual, smaller queries that would incur more overhead. Similarly, it may recommend more efficient database indexing strategies, caching frequently accessed data, or introducing background processing for time-consuming tasks.

These advanced optimizations are essential in ensuring that your application can handle the demands of real-world use, scaling to handle large datasets and high traffic volumes without suffering from performance bottlenecks.

For experienced developers, Cursor AI is not just a tool for writing code—it's a powerful assistant that helps refine every aspect of the development process. From unlocking advanced AI features that understand the intricacies of your project, to debugging code before it reaches production and optimizing for performance, Cursor AI allows developers to focus on the creative aspects of software development while leaving the tedious, repetitive, and error-prone tasks to the AI.

By integrating Cursor AI into your workflow, you can increase the efficiency, quality, and scalability of your code, allowing you to solve complex problems faster and more effectively. Whether you're working on small, high-performance applications or large, enterprise-level systems, Cursor AI offers the advanced features and capabilities needed to bring your software to the next level.

CHAPTER FIVE

Debugging   Smarter: AI-Driven
Troubleshooting

The process of debugging has long been one of the most challenging and time-consuming aspects of software development. As developers, we know that bugs are an inevitable part of creating software. What separates great developers from the rest is not the absence of bugs, but their ability to find and fix them efficiently. Traditional debugging methods—relying on manual inspection of code, print statements, and error logs—have served developers for decades. However, as the complexity of systems grows and applications scale, these methods often become insufficient.

This is where AI-driven troubleshooting begins to shine. With the rise of advanced AI tools like Cursor AI, developers are gaining access to a new era of debugging that is faster, more efficient, and, above all, smarter. The AI behind tools like Cursor AI doesn't just identify errors but proactively suggests fixes, analyzes code in real-time, and helps developers maintain high-quality code throughout the lifecycle of the project. This chapter explores how AI identifies and solves problems, the power of real-time error detection, and how developers can enhance their code quality using AI-powered suggestions.

> How AI Identifies and Solves Problems

At its core, AI-driven debugging isn't just about finding bugs; it's about understanding the context of the code and its behavior. Traditional debuggers rely on static patterns to spot errors, whereas Cursor AI takes a more dynamic approach. It constantly analyzes your code as you write it, recognizing potential issues before they even become apparent in the final product.

Cursor AI employs machine learning models trained on vast amounts of code from open-source projects, helping it understand patterns of good and bad code. It learns from this data and applies this knowledge to your project. For instance, if you're writing a function that interacts with an external API, Cursor AI will flag issues such as improper error handling, poor data sanitization, or inefficient data parsing. More than just catching syntax errors, it recognizes structural problems, logic flaws, and common pitfalls, providing insights based on real-world usage and best practices.

The AI goes a step further by analyzing how your code interacts with other parts of the application. In a large project, it's not enough to spot an error in one function. A bug in one section might cascade and affect other modules. Cursor AI can trace dependencies across the entire codebase, identifying where a problem originates and how it propagates. This allows the AI to suggest more holistic fixes rather than just a quick patch to the immediate issue. For instance, if a function is returning inconsistent results, Cursor AI may suggest not only fixing the function but also reviewing the inputs or dependencies that feed into it.

What makes Cursor AI even more powerful is its ability to continuously learn from the changes you make. As you fix bugs, it refines its suggestions, understanding your preferred patterns and adapting its advice accordingly. Over time, it becomes more attuned to the specifics of your project, offering increasingly relevant and efficient solutions to your problems.

> Real-Time Error Detection and Fixes

One of the most significant improvements AI brings to debugging is its ability to detect and resolve errors in real time. In traditional debugging, an error might only become apparent when you run the program, leaving you to sift through error logs or crash reports to identify the issue. With AI-driven debugging, errors are detected and highlighted as you type, allowing you to address issues as they arise rather than letting them accumulate over time.

Cursor AI operates as a real-time code monitor, scanning for potential errors as you write. It can identify issues like uninitialized variables, potential null pointer exceptions, improper use of data structures, and more. What makes this real-time detection particularly powerful is its proactive nature. Rather than waiting for the program to execute and crash, Cursor AI stops errors before they happen, providing immediate feedback and suggestions. For instance, if you're writing a function that's meant to parse data from an external file, Cursor AI will instantly recognize if the code has the potential to fail in certain situations. Perhaps you've forgotten to handle a scenario where the file is empty or incorrectly formatted. Rather than waiting for the code to fail, Cursor AI will flag the potential issue immediately and suggest how to handle it gracefully.

What sets Cursor AI apart is not just its ability to identify problems but also to suggest immediate fixes. The AI doesn't just point out errors in isolation; it offers contextual fixes based on what you're trying to achieve. For example, if a function isn't returning the correct results, Cursor AI might suggest a better algorithm, or if there's an issue with concurrency, it might propose synchronization techniques to handle multi-threading more effectively.

This ability to provide real-time fixes is especially valuable during the development cycle when bugs tend to accumulate quickly. With Cursor AI, developers can avoid the need for exhaustive post-mortem debugging sessions. Instead, they can fix errors as they work, preventing them from snowballing into more significant issues down the road.

> Enhancing Code Quality with AI-Powered Suggestions

While debugging is critical to software development, the ultimate goal is not just to eliminate bugs but to create high-quality, maintainable code. This is where Cursor AI's suggestions can make a substantial difference. AI-powered suggestions are not limited to detecting errors—they also help you improve your code's structure, readability, and efficiency.

One of the core strengths of Cursor AI is its ability to provide style and structure recommendations. While experienced developers understand the importance of writing clean, readable code, it can sometimes be difficult to maintain consistency throughout a large project. With AI-powered suggestions, Cursor AI can recommend improvements such as better variable naming conventions, more efficient data structures, or improved algorithmic approaches.

For example, consider a scenario where you're working with a loop that performs a repetitive operation multiple times. Cursor AI might suggest converting that loop into a more efficient data structure or propose using a higher-level function that's both easier to understand and more efficient. It might also point out where you've written overly complex functions and suggest breaking them into smaller, more manageable ones. These suggestions not only improve the quality of the code but also make it more maintainable in the long term.

Another area where Cursor AI excels is in the optimization of performance. Writing fast and efficient code is one of the primary concerns for experienced developers, especially when dealing with large datasets or high-performance applications. Cursor AI can analyze your code and recommend optimizations that reduce complexity, lower memory usage, or improve computational efficiency. It might recommend replacing a nested loop with a more efficient algorithm or suggest better ways to handle data storage and retrieval. But the AI-powered suggestions go even further by focusing on best practices. As software systems grow, developers can easily overlook small issues that could affect the maintainability and scalability of the code in the future. Cursor AI ensures that your code adheres to the best practices by recommending improvements to your overall coding style, security practices, and error handling mechanisms.

> The Future of Debugging: Smarter, Faster, and More Efficient

The advent of AI-driven debugging tools like Cursor AI marks a significant turning point in the development process. By providing real-time feedback, proactive error detection, and intelligent suggestions, Cursor AI helps developers troubleshoot and optimize their code more efficiently than ever before. It doesn't just identify issues; it actively contributes to the process of writing better, more reliable code, making it an indispensable tool for modern software development.

The future of debugging, it seems, lies in collaboration between developers and intelligent systems. Rather than spending hours hunting for elusive bugs or trying to remember obscure syntax rules, developers can rely on Cursor AI to spot issues, suggest fixes, and optimize their codebase, allowing them to focus on what truly matters: building robust, innovative software. As AI continues to evolve, its ability to assist developers in even more complex tasks will only improve. With the combination of real-time error detection, context-aware fixes, and intelligent suggestions, Cursor AI is not just making debugging smarter—it's making the entire process of software development more intuitive, efficient, and enjoyable.

CHAPTER SIX

Collaborating with AI: Enhancing Team Productivity

Software development is often a team endeavor. The complexity of modern applications demands collaboration among developers, testers, designers, and product managers. This collaborative environment brings its own challenges. Multiple people working on different aspects of the same codebase can quickly lead to inconsistent code quality, missed bugs, and overlooked best practices. As the number of developers in a project increases, maintaining a smooth and efficient workflow becomes progressively difficult.

This is where Cursor AI steps in, transforming not only individual productivity but also the dynamics of team collaboration. Whether you're working with a small team or a large enterprise, the tools and strategies enabled by Cursor AI enhance the collaborative process, ensuring that teams stay productive, consistent, and efficient throughout the entire software development lifecycle. In this chapter, we explore how Cursor AI enhances team coding efforts, how it accelerates and automates the code review process, and the best practices for collaborative development using Cursor AI.

> How Cursor AI Enhances Team Coding Efforts

When multiple developers contribute to the same codebase, consistency is often the first casualty. With each developer bringing their own style, preferences, and experience, maintaining a cohesive approach to coding can be difficult. Over time, these inconsistencies can lead to confusion, bugs, and inefficiencies. Cursor AI directly addresses this issue by creating a unified coding experience across the entire team. It ensures that all developers follow the same coding standards, structure, and best practices, regardless of their individual backgrounds. When a team is using Cursor AI, the AI acts as a guide, making sure that suggestions, refactorings, and fixes are consistent with the team's coding guidelines.

For instance, if one developer prefers more compact, efficient code while another favors a more explicit, verbose approach, Cursor AI will be able to suggest solutions that align with the project's established coding style. This reduces the friction between team members, allowing developers to focus on solving problems rather than discussing coding styles or troubleshooting inconsistencies. Moreover, Cursor AI is an ideal tool for ensuring that code is not only functional but also scalable and maintainable. As developers write new features or fix bugs, Cursor AI ensures that any changes align with the broader architecture and vision of the project. It alerts developers to potential issues like code duplication or inefficient algorithms and provides suggestions for improvement that align with team standards.

The ability of Cursor AI to provide consistent and context-aware recommendations fosters smoother collaboration, ensuring that every developer contributes to a high-quality codebase. It serves as an intelligent assistant that provides real-time support, ensuring that team productivity is maximized and that everyone is working toward the same goals.

> AI for Code Reviews: Automating and Accelerating the Process

One of the most critical and time-consuming activities in a team development process is the code review. Traditionally, code reviews have been a manual, tedious process—one that often takes a considerable amount of time, particularly for larger teams or complex codebases. A thorough code review involves not only looking for bugs but also checking for adherence to coding standards, ensuring that the code is efficient, maintainable, and properly documented. With the increasing demands of rapid development cycles, this process can quickly become a bottleneck, slowing down progress.

Cursor AI transforms this process by automating and accelerating many aspects of the code review. Rather than relying solely on human reviewers to catch every possible error, Cursor AI steps in as a first line of defense. It scans code for syntax errors, adherence to coding standards, and potential logical flaws, providing immediate feedback. This allows human reviewers to focus on higher-level concerns like design, architecture, and functionality rather than sifting through code for minor issues.

In addition to detecting issues, Cursor AI can also suggest specific improvements. For example, if a function is inefficient or written in a non-idiomatic way, the AI will suggest a more optimal or cleaner version. If there are areas where the code could be refactored for better readability, Cursor AI will point them out. These suggestions make the code review process more efficient, reducing the need for back-and-forth comments and speeding up the overall review cycle.

For teams that rely on continuous integration and delivery (CI/CD), Cursor AI can be integrated into the CI pipeline, automatically reviewing pull requests as they are submitted. This ensures that code is reviewed immediately after it's written, eliminating delays in the development process. Rather than waiting for a team member to manually review a piece of code, the AI ensures that all contributions meet quality standards before they are merged into the main branch.

This automation doesn't just save time; it also improves the overall quality of the codebase. By providing real-time, consistent feedback, Cursor AI ensures that code quality remains high throughout the entire development process. Developers are empowered to write better code from the outset, and the code review process becomes more about refining the solution rather than fixing avoidable mistakes.

> Best Practices for Collaborative Development Using Cursor AI

To get the most out of Cursor AI in a team setting, there are several best practices that developers should follow. These practices ensure that Cursor AI functions as an integral part of the development workflow, enhancing collaboration and streamlining productivity.

1.Establish Clear Coding Guidelines

While Cursor AI helps standardize code, it's important for teams to first establish clear coding standards and guidelines. This ensures that the AI suggestions align with the overall team approach. Whether it's naming conventions, formatting styles, or preferred design patterns, having a unified approach allows Cursor AI to make consistent suggestions that reflect the team's goals and preferences.

2. Integrate Cursor AI into the Development Workflow

To maximize the benefits of Cursor AI, integrate it directly into the development environment and CI/CD pipeline. Tools like Visual Studio Code, JetBrains, and GitHub all support integrations with Cursor AI, ensuring that developers get real-time feedback as they write code. This integration streamlines the process, making it easy to catch issues early and ensure that every piece of code that gets merged meets team standards.

3. Encourage Collaboration Through Code Reviews

While Cursor AI automates much of the code review process, it's still important for developers to collaborate and discuss design decisions. Use Cursor AI as a supplement to human review, not a replacement. AI should handle the repetitive tasks, such as checking for syntax or performance issues, while developers focus on the larger aspects of the code such as design and architecture. This collaboration ensures that the team is always moving forward while maintaining high standards.

4.Leverage AI-Powered Suggestions for Learning and Improvement

One of the key benefits of using Cursor AI in a team environment is that it provides a constant feedback loop. Developers, particularly those who are less experienced, can use AI-powered suggestions as learning opportunities. By understanding why Cursor AI recommends certain changes, team members can improve their coding practices and learn from the insights it provides. Over time, this will elevate the overall skill level of the entire team.

5.Regularly Review and Update AI-Generated Suggestions

Although Cursor AI is powerful, it's important for teams to periodically review the suggestions it provides to ensure they still align with the evolving needs of the project. As a team grows and the project matures, new coding standards may emerge, or priorities might shift. Ensuring that Cursor AI stays aligned with the team's changing needs allows the AI to remain a valuable asset throughout the project's lifecycle.

Cursor AI has the potential to revolutionize the way development teams collaborate, automating repetitive tasks, accelerating the code review process, and ensuring consistent, high-quality code. By integrating Cursor AI into the development workflow, teams can increase productivity, reduce errors, and maintain higher standards of software quality.

When used correctly, Cursor AI doesn't replace the need for human collaboration— it enhances it, allowing developers to spend less time fixing problems and more time solving complex, creative challenges. Whether you are working in a small team or an enterprise setting, Cursor AI acts as a powerful ally in streamlining the development process, ensuring that the focus remains on building robust, scalable, and maintainable software.

CHAPTER SEVEN

Future-Proofing Your Career with Cursor AI

The landscape of technology is in constant flux, with new tools, languages, and paradigms emerging at a relentless pace. For software developers, this creates both a challenge and an opportunity. As new technologies rise, those who don't adapt risk falling behind, while those who embrace the future have the chance to lead the charge. One of the most significant advancements in recent years is the integration of artificial intelligence into development tools. These AI-powered tools are reshaping the way developers write, debug, and optimize code. One such tool, Cursor AI, is at the forefront of this transformation.

For developers, the future is clear: AI is not just an add-on, but a vital component of the development workflow. In this chapter, we'll explore why learning AI-assisted development is essential for career growth, how to integrate AI into your workflow for long-term success, and the career opportunities that await those who stay ahead of the curve.

> Why Learning AI-Assisted Development is Key to Career Growth

As software development continues to evolve, one of the most noticeable changes is the growing reliance on artificial intelligence in the development process. While AI-assisted development tools like Cursor AI may have seemed like novelties just a few years ago, they are now becoming mainstream. For a developer, mastering AI-powered tools is no longer optional—it's necessary to remain competitive in a fast-moving industry.

At its core, AI-assisted development improves efficiency and quality, two critical factors that any developer will need to succeed. Cursor AI helps developers write code more quickly, identify potential bugs before they become problems, and offer optimization suggestions that might otherwise go unnoticed. As these tools continue to improve, the need for human developers to manually code every line of an application diminishes. The future of software development lies in the ability to collaborate with AI, using its capabilities to augment human intelligence rather than replace it.

For developers, understanding how to leverage AI-powered tools is an investment in long-term career growth. The skills required to work with AI-assisted development tools will become increasingly valuable, as more companies adopt these technologies to enhance their development processes. In fact, developers who are skilled in using AI tools will likely find themselves in high demand, as they will be able to increase productivity and reduce the risk of errors, making them indispensable assets to any development team. Learning how to harness the power of tools like Cursor AI is not just about enhancing your technical skillset; it's also about positioning yourself as a forward-thinking professional in an ever-changing industry. As AI becomes an integral part of software development, those who can seamlessly integrate AI into their workflows will be better prepared for the challenges and opportunities that the future holds.

> **Integrating AI into Your Workflow for Long-Term Success**

Adopting Cursor AI into your development workflow isn't just about using a new tool;

it's about changing the way you approach your entire coding process. The most successful developers understand that the key to integrating AI into their workflow is a mindset shift—moving from writing code in isolation to collaborating with a tool that can enhance their work at every stage.

The first step in integrating AI into your workflow is understanding how Cursor AI fits into your existing tools. It's important to recognize that Cursor AI doesn't replace your development environment, but rather enhances it. Whether you're using Visual Studio Code, JetBrains, or any other popular code editor, Cursor AI can seamlessly integrate into your environment to provide real-time suggestions, detect errors before they surface, and offer refactoring tips that improve the quality of your code.

Once integrated, the next step is to start relying on Cursor AI for its intelligent suggestions. Instead of manually checking for errors or figuring out the most efficient way to write a function, let Cursor AI handle those tasks for you. Its suggestions will speed up the process and provide you with insights that might take much longer to discover on your own. As you get more accustomed to using Cursor AI, you'll start to rely on its recommendations more heavily, allowing you to focus on solving more complex problems, rather than getting bogged down in the repetitive aspects of coding.

However, relying on AI tools doesn't mean completely stepping away from the fundamental aspects of software development. The best developers understand that Cursor AI is a tool to be used in conjunction with their own expertise. The AI provides suggestions, but it is ultimately up to the developer to evaluate those suggestions and determine which ones align with the goals of the project. This balance of human creativity and AI-powered efficiency is the key to long-term success. For developers looking to future-proof their careers, embracing AI is crucial. The ability to integrate AI into your workflow will set you apart from other developers who may still be hesitant to adopt these tools. As AI tools become more sophisticated, developers who can seamlessly incorporate them into their process will be able to deliver higher-quality software faster and more efficiently. The future of software development isn't just about writing code—it's about collaborating with intelligent tools that enhance your capabilities and help you solve problems more effectively.

Staying Ahead of the Curve: Career Opportunities in AI-Powered Development

As the use of AI in development becomes more widespread, new career opportunities are emerging for developers who are skilled in AI-assisted tools. For developers who are looking to stay ahead of the curve, understanding the potential applications of AI in software development is essential.

One key area where AI is revolutionizing development is in automated testing and quality assurance. Traditionally, testing has been a time-consuming process, with developers manually writing test cases and debugging code. However, AI tools like Cursor AI can automate many aspects of testing, from identifying bugs to suggesting test cases based on the code written. Developers who can work with AI-powered testing tools will be in high demand, as they can help companies improve their testing processes and reduce the risk of bugs reaching production.

Another exciting area is AI-driven optimization. As more companies seek to build scalable, high-performance applications, developers who understand how to use AI to optimize their code will be well-positioned to take advantage of new opportunities. AI can help developers identify performance bottlenecks, recommend more efficient algorithms, and suggest ways to optimize memory usage. Developers with expertise in these areas will be able to contribute to the development of more robust, high-performance systems, making them valuable assets to any company focused on innovation.

Finally, there is an increasing demand for AI specialists in software development. As AI becomes a more integral part of the development process, companies are looking for developers who have a deep understanding of machine learning algorithms, natural language processing, and other AI techniques. These specialists will be responsible for building and fine-tuning the AI models that power tools like Cursor AI, and will play a crucial role in advancing the capabilities of AI-powered development tools.

The future of software development is undeniably linked to AI, and developers who are proficient in AI-assisted tools will have a significant competitive advantage. Those who embrace these tools early on and integrate them into their workflows will be able to position themselves as leaders in the field, opening up new career opportunities and ensuring long-term success.

AI-powered development tools like Cursor AI are reshaping the way software is built. For developers, embracing these tools is no longer just a matter of keeping up with the latest trends—it's a matter of securing their place in the future of software development. Learning how to integrate AI into your workflow, leveraging its capabilities to enhance productivity, and staying ahead of the curve will be essential for long-term career growth. As AI continues to evolve, developers who can collaborate with these intelligent tools will be at the forefront of innovation, creating high-quality, efficient software and leading the charge into the next era of technology.

CHAPTER EIGHT

Case Studies: Leading Companies Using Cursor AI

In the fast-paced world of software development, staying ahead of the competition requires more than just writing clean, functional code. It demands the ability to work smarter, optimize workflows, and leverage the latest technologies to increase efficiency and scalability. One of the most transformative technologies in this regard is artificial intelligence. As AI becomes increasingly integrated into development workflows, it is reshaping how companies build software, manage projects, and deliver products. In this chapter, we explore how some of the most innovative companies in the tech industry—Shopify, OpenAI, and Instacart—are using Cursor AI to streamline their development processes, improve efficiency, and scale their operations.

>Shopify: Building Software Faster and Smarter

As one of the leading e-commerce platforms globally, Shopify has to constantly innovate and adapt to meet the needs of its diverse customer base. The company's development teams are tasked with building a highly reliable and scalable platform that can handle millions of transactions daily. For a company of Shopify's size and scope, improving development efficiency isn't just about writing code faster—it's about writing smarter code, ensuring that every piece of software released is of the highest quality, and maintaining a robust platform that can scale seamlessly as the company grows.

Cursor AI plays a crucial role in Shopify's software development process, helping developers streamline their workflows and reduce the time spent on repetitive tasks. With Cursor AI integrated into their IDEs, developers at Shopify benefit from real-time code suggestions, error detection, and intelligent refactoring tools that help them write cleaner and more efficient code. The AI's ability to analyze large codebases and provide context-aware suggestions ensures that developers can build software more quickly and with fewer errors, thus reducing the time it takes to get new features and improvements into production. One of the key ways Cursor AI has helped Shopify is by automating repetitive coding tasks. Instead of developers manually writing boilerplate code, Cursor AI can automatically generate common structures or identify areas where code can be optimized. This has allowed Shopify's developers to focus more on solving complex, high-impact problems, while the AI takes care of the mundane and repetitive tasks. As a result, Shopify has been able to significantly speed up the development process without compromising on quality.

Additionally, Cursor AI's ability to assist with debugging and error detection has helped Shopify maintain the high performance and reliability of its platform. With real-time feedback on potential issues and suggestions for fixes, developers can address problems early in the development cycle, reducing the likelihood of bugs slipping through the cracks and affecting the user experience.

>OpenAI: Leveraging AI to Improve Efficiency

At OpenAI, the company's mission is to ensure that artificial intelligence benefits all of humanity. As a research and development organization at the cutting edge of AI, OpenAI is focused not only on advancing the capabilities of AI models but also on improving how AI is used to solve real-world problems. With its commitment to pushing the boundaries of what's possible with AI, OpenAI also understands the importance of leveraging AI to enhance its own internal processes, particularly in software development.

For OpenAI, Cursor AI is a key tool in helping developers build, optimize, and refine the AI systems that power its groundbreaking research. The AI-driven features of Cursor AI assist OpenAI's engineers in maintaining the efficiency of their workflows and ensuring that they can tackle complex problems with the highest level of productivity. One of the most valuable aspects of Cursor AI for OpenAI is its ability to handle large, complex codebases. As a company that works on cutting-edge AI research, OpenAI's code often involves intricate algorithms, data pipelines, and machine learning models that require careful attention to detail.

Cursor AI supports OpenAI's engineers by offering context-aware suggestions that streamline the coding process and ensure that best practices are followed. For instance, Cursor AI can automatically detect potential performance bottlenecks in machine learning models and suggest optimizations, saving valuable time and allowing developers to focus on refining the models themselves. Additionally, Cursor AI's error detection and debugging features help OpenAI's engineers identify issues early in the development cycle, which is critical when building systems that need to operate at scale and maintain high levels of performance. With Cursor AI handling many of the routine tasks associated with code writing, refactoring, and debugging, OpenAI's developers are able to accelerate their work and maintain the high standards of quality that are expected of a leader in AI research. The integration of Cursor AI into

OpenAI's workflow has ultimately contributed to the company's ability to advance AI technology more quickly and efficiently.

>Instacart: How AI Transformed Their Development Process

Instacart, the popular grocery delivery service, has revolutionized the way people shop for food and household items. As a company that provides real-time delivery of groceries, Instacart needs to maintain a fast and efficient development process to support its rapidly growing user base. With millions of customers relying on the platform every day, it's crucial that Instacart's software development teams are able to release features and updates quickly while maintaining high performance and reliability.

In a fast-paced environment like Instacart's, Cursor AI has become an essential tool for enhancing development productivity and ensuring that the company's software remains scalable and high-performing. Cursor AI helps Instacart's engineers manage the complexity of their large-scale systems by providing real-time feedback, context-aware code suggestions, and intelligent refactorings. The AI's ability to analyze code in real-time and suggest improvements has been particularly valuable in helping Instacart's developers keep up with the demands of rapid feature releases and ongoing system optimizations.

One of the ways Cursor AI has helped Instacart is by automating many of the repetitive tasks associated with building and maintaining large-scale applications. For example, Cursor AI can suggest optimizations for database queries, refactor inefficient code, and generate boilerplate code for common functions. This automation has allowed Instacart's developers to focus more on solving high-level architectural problems and creating innovative features for their users.

Moreover, Cursor AI's error detection capabilities have been instrumental in helping Instacart catch bugs early in the development process. With real-time error detection and contextual fixes, developers can address issues before they reach production, ensuring that Instacart's platform remains stable and reliable for users. The AI's proactive approach to identifying potential bugs or performance bottlenecks has saved Instacart valuable time and resources, allowing the company to focus on scaling its operations and expanding its offerings.

The case studies of Shopify, OpenAI, and Instacart highlight the transformative potential of AI-assisted development tools like Cursor AI. Whether it's enhancing team productivity, speeding up the software development process, or maintaining the highest standards of quality, these companies are leveraging AI to gain a competitive edge in their respective industries.

As we continue to move toward a more AI-driven future, it's clear that the companies that embrace these tools will not only improve their development processes but also remain at the forefront of innovation. The integration of AI into software development is not a passing trend—it is a fundamental shift that will define the next generation of software engineering. For developers, understanding how to work with AI tools like Cursor AI is essential to staying relevant in an increasingly complex and competitive field.

CHAPTER NINE

Customizing Cursor AI to Fit Your Needs

In the realm of software development, the tools you use can have a profound impact on both your productivity and the quality of your work. For developers who are accustomed to tailoring their environments, the idea of customizing a development tool like Cursor AI is a natural next step in achieving peak efficiency. Cursor AI is not a one-size-fits-all solution. Its true potential is unlocked when it is tailored to fit your unique coding style, workflow, and team requirements. This chapter explores how developers can customize Cursor AI to enhance their coding experience, improve workflow efficiency, and create an environment that matches their needs, whether working solo or within a team. By understanding the flexibility of Cursor AI, you can adjust its behavior to reflect your preferences and integrate it seamlessly into your development process.

> Tailoring Cursor AI to Your Coding Style

Every developer has their own approach to coding, shaped by experience, project requirements, and personal preferences. Whether you prefer writing concise, functional code or a more verbose and explanatory style, Cursor AI is built with the flexibility to adapt to your specific coding habits. Customizing the AI to your coding style allows you to maintain a sense of ownership over your development process, while still taking advantage of the efficiency enhancements it offers.

The first step in customizing Cursor AI is understanding how it learns and adapts to your code. Unlike basic autocompletion tools, Cursor AI analyzes your existing codebase to identify patterns and predict what you are likely to write next. Over time, it learns from the way you structure your functions, variables, and algorithms, becoming increasingly adept at suggesting relevant code.

If you prefer short, clean one-liners, Cursor AI will adapt by suggesting concise, efficient snippets. Conversely, if you lean toward more detailed, explicit code with descriptive variable names and careful formatting, the AI will align with your style. By providing suggestions that reflect your preferences, Cursor AI reduces the cognitive load of remembering syntax and patterns, allowing you to focus on solving problems rather than formatting code.

Additionally, Cursor AI can be configured to offer suggestions based on specific programming paradigms, such as object-oriented programming or functional programming. If you tend to favor one approach over another, the AI can be adjusted to recommend methods, classes, or functions that fit the paradigm you're using, further enhancing your productivity.

This ability to tailor suggestions to your coding style fosters a more intuitive, frictionless experience, where Cursor AI acts as an intelligent assistant that feels like a natural extension of your coding habits.

> Adjusting AI Suggestions for Maximum Efficiency

While Cursor AI is built to make intelligent recommendations, not all suggestions will be relevant or helpful for every project. As your development environment and projects evolve, you may find that some of the AI's suggestions are better suited to certain tasks than others. The beauty of Cursor AI lies in its ability to be finely tuned to maximize efficiency and reduce distractions.

The settings menu in Cursor AI allows you to adjust how aggressive or subtle the AI's suggestions are. For developers who prefer less interruption, suggestions can be made more subtle, appearing only when the AI is fairly certain of the most relevant next step. Alternatively, for developers who appreciate more hands-on assistance, suggestions can be more frequent, appearing with each keystroke or when a potential inefficiency is detected.

Another useful feature of Cursor AI is its ability to filter suggestions based on the context of the project or task at hand. For example, if you are working on a web application, Cursor AI can prioritize suggestions related to front-end technologies like HTML, CSS, or JavaScript, and focus less on back-end languages or libraries that aren't relevant. By narrowing the focus of suggestions, Cursor AI becomes more efficient, saving you time and helping you stay within the scope of the project.

Additionally, Cursor AI allows you to configure which types of code should be prioritized. For example, if you value performance over readability in certain areas, you can adjust the AI to focus on optimizing the code for speed and efficiency. Conversely, if maintainability and readability are higher priorities, the AI can be tuned to suggest more modular, readable code, even if it sacrifices some efficiency.

These adjustments make Cursor AI a tool that enhances, rather than overwhelms, the development process. By fine-tuning how the AI interacts with your workflow, you can make suggestions that truly align with your goals, reducing distractions and improving overall efficiency.

> Fine-Tuning Settings for Personal or Team Use

While Cursor AI offers significant flexibility for individual developers, the ability to customize its settings for team use is equally important. In a team setting, collaboration and consistency are key. With multiple developers working on the same codebase, ensuring that everyone adheres to the same standards and practices can be a challenge. Fortunately, Cursor AI offers features that enable teams to maintain uniformity while also allowing for personal customization. For teams, Cursor AI can be configured to enforce team-wide coding standards. This ensures that all team members, regardless of their individual preferences, write code that aligns with the team's overall structure and guidelines. Whether it's using a specific indentation style, following naming conventions, or adhering to particular architectural principles, Cursor AI can help maintain consistency across the codebase by automatically suggesting the correct style for each developer.

At the same time, Cursor AI doesn't stifle personal preferences. Developers can still adjust their individual settings within the team framework, ensuring that their personal coding style is respected while still adhering to the broader team guidelines. For example, a developer might prefer using camelCase for variable names while the team uses snake_case for function names. Cursor AI can be configured to automatically adjust for these personal preferences without causing conflicts with the team's conventions.

For larger teams, Cursor AI also provides tools for managing team workflows and ensuring that code quality is maintained across different branches and pull requests. The AI can automatically flag potential issues in code reviews, ensuring that suggestions align with team standards, even before the code is merged. This helps avoid the need for lengthy back-and-forth discussions over coding practices and focuses the team's efforts on solving the more complex aspects of the project.

Moreover, for teams working with agile methodologies or continuous integration systems, Cursor AI can be integrated into the CI pipeline to automatically check for code quality and adherence to team standards as developers submit their work. This integration ensures that every piece of code is validated in real time, preventing inconsistencies or errors from accumulating over the course of the development process.

The true power of Cursor AI lies in its ability to adapt to your personal coding style, integrate seamlessly into your workflow, and scale to meet the needs of larger teams. By tailoring Cursor AI to your preferences and team standards, you can maximize its value and unlock a more efficient, productive, and collaborative development process. Whether you're a solo developer looking to work smarter or part of a large team aiming for consistency and efficiency, Cursor AI offers the tools to help you achieve your goals. As development practices evolve, tools like Cursor AI will continue to play a critical role in shaping the future of software engineering. Customizing the AI to fit your needs is the first step toward unlocking its full potential and

ensuring that you and your team stay ahead
of the curve.

CHAPTER TEN

Preparing for the Future: The Next Evolution of Cursor AI

The world of software development is one that never stands still. In recent years, the introduction of artificial intelligence tools into development workflows has ushered in a new era of productivity and efficiency. Tools like Cursor AI are pushing the boundaries of what developers can achieve, but as technology evolves, so too must the tools that drive it. The journey of Cursor AI is far from over. As AI continues to mature and learn from vast datasets, its capabilities will grow, transforming the way we write, debug, and optimize code. In this chapter, we explore what's next for AI in development, the upcoming features of Cursor AI that will revolutionize how we work, and the importance of continuous learning and adaptation in an ever-changing tech landscape.

>What's Next for AI in Development?

Artificial intelligence in software development is not a passing trend; it is a fundamental shift in how we approach problem-solving, code generation, and system design. The rise of Cursor AI is a testament to how quickly AI can change the development process, but this is just the beginning. As the AI's understanding of code deepens and its learning algorithms improve, we can expect to see more profound innovations that will change the way developers interact with their environments.

One of the most significant advancements on the horizon is the increased ability of AI to generate entire software systems based on high-level instructions. Currently, Cursor AI assists developers by suggesting code, detecting errors, and offering refactoring suggestions. However, future versions of Cursor AI could evolve to assist in the generation of entire frameworks, libraries, or even fully functional applications, based solely on project specifications. Imagine describing a project's requirements to Cursor AI, and having the AI autonomously create the code necessary to bring that vision to life. This level of assistance would enable developers to focus more on strategic decisions and less on mundane tasks, significantly increasing productivity.

Additionally, Cursor AI's role in debugging and error detection will likely become even more powerful. In the future, AI will not just identify and fix simple coding errors, but will also anticipate complex issues such as performance bottlenecks, security vulnerabilities, or scalability challenges. It will analyze entire systems to predict potential failure points, offering solutions before they even arise. This proactive approach to problem-solving will fundamentally change how we build and maintain software.

Another exciting possibility is the integration of AI with cloud-based environments and containerized applications. As cloud computing becomes more integral to modern development, Cursor AI will likely expand its capabilities to optimize cloud-based resources, manage deployment strategies, and enhance collaboration in distributed environments. The ability to seamlessly integrate AI into cloud-native architectures will make it possible to automate everything from resource management to version control, providing developers with unparalleled efficiency and flexibility.

>Upcoming Features and How They'll Change the Game

The evolution of Cursor AI doesn't end with improved code suggestions and error detection. As the platform continues to grow, several new features will be introduced that will take the development process to the next level.

1.Contextual Code Generation

One of the most anticipated features is enhanced contextual code generation. Currently, Cursor AI excels at making suggestions based on the code already written, but with future updates, the AI will be able to understand higher-level concepts. For example, if you are building an e-commerce platform, Cursor AI could generate full-featured modules like payment gateways, product catalogs, and user authentication systems with a deep understanding of your project's requirements. This will save time and reduce errors, as developers will no longer have to manually write complex, repetitive code from scratch.

2.Collaborative AI

As development teams continue to grow, collaboration becomes more important than ever. Cursor AI will evolve to include collaborative features that enable seamless teamwork. With real-time feedback, developers working on the same project will be able to see AI suggestions and corrections simultaneously, ensuring consistency across the team. Collaborative features could include shared AI insights, standardized code suggestions, and the ability to align on best practices in real-time, making it easier to maintain cohesion in large-scale projects.

3.Automated Testing and QA

Testing and quality assurance (QA) are essential parts of the software development process, but they can be time-consuming and often neglected. The future of Cursor AI will involve tighter integration with automated testing frameworks, allowing the AI to generate unit tests, perform code analysis for potential vulnerabilities, and run performance simulations automatically. AI will be able to identify edge cases that a developer might miss, ensuring that the software is robust and scalable before it reaches production. This feature will not only enhance the quality of the code but also reduce the time spent on manual testing, accelerating the development cycle.

4.Cross-Language and Multi-Platform Support

As the demand for multi-platform applications increases, Cursor AI will continue to improve its ability to work across different programming languages and platforms. Whether it's mobile, web, or desktop development, the AI will be able to offer suggestions tailored to the specific platform, making it easier for developers to work in different environments without needing to be experts in each one. This level of flexibility will make Cursor AI an indispensable tool for developers working in today's multi-faceted technology ecosystem.

>Staying Ahead with Continuous Learning and Adaptation

As Cursor AI continues to evolve, developers must adopt a mindset of continuous learning and adaptation. AI is a rapidly advancing field, and staying at the forefront requires that developers not only use the tools available but also understand how to leverage them effectively.

One of the keys to staying ahead in this AI-driven world is investing in personal growth and adaptability. Developers who embrace new technologies, keep up with the latest trends, and understand the principles behind the tools they use will be better positioned to take advantage of the next wave of innovation. Understanding the intricacies of machine learning algorithms, natural language processing, and AI programming paradigms will help developers unlock the full potential of AI tools like Cursor AI.

Moreover, as AI continues to integrate into software development workflows, developers must learn how to collaborate effectively with these intelligent tools. Just as developers have adapted to working with IDEs, version control systems, and cloud environments, they will need to learn how to incorporate AI into their day-to-day work. This includes understanding when to rely on AI suggestions, how to refine and personalize those suggestions, and how to use AI to tackle higher-level problems.

The key to staying competitive in the age of AI is to view these tools as collaborative partners rather than replacements. As AI continues to develop, those who can seamlessly integrate these tools into their workflows will thrive in a rapidly changing landscape.

The next evolution of Cursor AI is a journey toward smarter, more efficient software development. With the ability to generate code, anticipate problems, automate testing, and foster collaboration, Cursor AI will continue to transform how developers work. By staying ahead of the curve, embracing new features, and committing to continuous learning, developers can harness the power of AI to enhance their careers and contribute to the future of technology. As the development world moves forward, those who adapt to and collaborate with AI will lead the charge in creating innovative, efficient, and scalable software.

CONCLUSION

The Future of Development is Now: Take Control with Cursor AI

The landscape of software development has undergone seismic shifts over the last few decades. What once relied on the manual, tedious process of writing code from scratch, meticulously debugging, and optimizing systems has evolved into a dynamic process where intelligent tools now collaborate with developers. Among the most revolutionary of these tools is Cursor AI. As we've explored throughout this guide, Cursor AI is more than just a tool—it's an evolution of how we approach coding, debugging, and even collaboration. It's a partner that empowers developers to work faster, smarter, and more efficiently.

The future of software development is no longer a distant concept—it's here, and it's being driven by AI tools like Cursor AI. For developers, this shift offers not just new possibilities but a mandate to adapt and evolve. The question is no longer whether AI will become an integral part of development—it already is. The real question is: how will you adapt to this new world?

> The Future of Development is Now: Take Control with Cursor AI

For years, software developers were tasked with writing every line of code by hand, debugging painstakingly, and optimizing each function for performance. This process, while rewarding, was also riddled with inefficiencies that slowed the pace of innovation. Cursor AI marks a dramatic shift in that approach, offering developers a smart assistant that streamlines many of the traditional challenges in coding and development.

The capabilities of Cursor AI extend far beyond what earlier development tools offered. Instead of simply providing syntax suggestions, Cursor AI integrates deeply into the development process by understanding code context and offering intelligent suggestions. Whether it's helping identify bugs before they even appear, suggesting refactorings for efficiency, or predicting the next line of code you're likely to write, Cursor AI offers unprecedented levels of support.

The future of development isn't about working harder—it's about working smarter. Cursor AI takes care of repetitive and tedious tasks, so developers can focus on the creative and strategic aspects of their work. By seamlessly integrating into your existing workflow, it ensures that your development process is both faster and more efficient. It's not simply about adding more tools to your arsenal—it's about transforming your entire approach to software development. In this new era, development is no longer isolated to the individual developer but a collaboration between human expertise and machine intelligence. For the forward-thinking developer, embracing Cursor AI is not a choice—it's an opportunity. The more you learn to harness the full power of this tool, the more you can unlock new ways to approach your work, solve complex problems, and become a leader in the field. The future of development is already here, and those who take control now will shape the next chapter of software creation.

> **Embrace AI and Transform Your Coding Career**

The integration of AI into software development is an inevitability. As artificial intelligence continues to evolve, so too will the ways we create software, from the very first line of code to deployment. This shift presents an exciting opportunity, but it also demands adaptation. Developers who embrace AI-powered tools like Cursor AI are positioning themselves for success in a rapidly changing industry.

Embracing AI does not mean abandoning the foundational skills that make a great developer—far from it. Rather, it's about augmenting those skills with powerful new tools that enhance productivity, improve code quality, and reduce errors. It's about building upon your knowledge of software design and leveraging AI to work more effectively. As AI continues to advance, developers will find that their roles will evolve to become more strategic and focused on problem-solving, rather than repetitive coding tasks.

By adopting AI tools now, developers can future-proof their careers, ensuring they remain relevant as the industry evolves. This is not just about coding faster—it's about becoming better developers. With Cursor AI, you're not simply optimizing your coding process; you're enhancing your ability to think critically, make high-level design decisions, and tackle more complex projects. For those who are just starting out in their coding journey, the integration of AI tools into the development process offers a unique advantage. It levels the playing field, providing new developers with access to tools that improve coding quality and reduce the time spent on debugging and optimization. Rather than spending hours learning the intricacies of a language, new developers can focus on understanding problem-solving strategies, architectural design, and the creative aspects of coding.

For seasoned developers, embracing AI is a chance to stay at the cutting edge of innovation. As the demand for AI expertise grows, those who can master AI-powered development tools will find themselves in high demand. Understanding how to use tools like Cursor AI will set you apart in a competitive job market, ensuring that you're not only keeping pace with changes in technology but driving them.

The integration of AI into development workflows presents developers with the opportunity to shift focus from time-consuming, repetitive tasks to the more innovative and high-level aspects of software creation. AI will continue to evolve, and as it does, it will open doors to new possibilities in the world of software development. Those who take advantage of these tools today will be in the best position to lead the charge into the future.

The future of software development is undeniably shaped by artificial intelligence. As tools like Cursor AI become more advanced, they will continue to redefine the way developers work, collaborate, and innovate. Rather than being seen as a passing trend, AI is a permanent shift that will fundamentally alter the development process.

For developers, this change presents both a challenge and an opportunity. To stay ahead of the curve, embracing AI is not just a way to remain competitive—it is essential for growth. The future of development is now, and with Cursor AI, developers can take control of this transformation, improving their workflow, enhancing their coding practices, and positioning themselves for success in an ever-evolving industry.

In the end, it's not just about writing code faster or more efficiently—it's about using AI to push the boundaries of what's possible in software development. By embracing AI and transforming the way we work, developers will not only thrive in the changing landscape but will shape the very future of technology itself.